Fun with Science

Primary Classroom Science Centers • At-Home Science Projects

Written by Timothy M. English and Gayla Irene English

Illustrated by Kathryn Marlin

Fearon Teacher Aids
A Division of Frank Schaffer Publications, Inc.

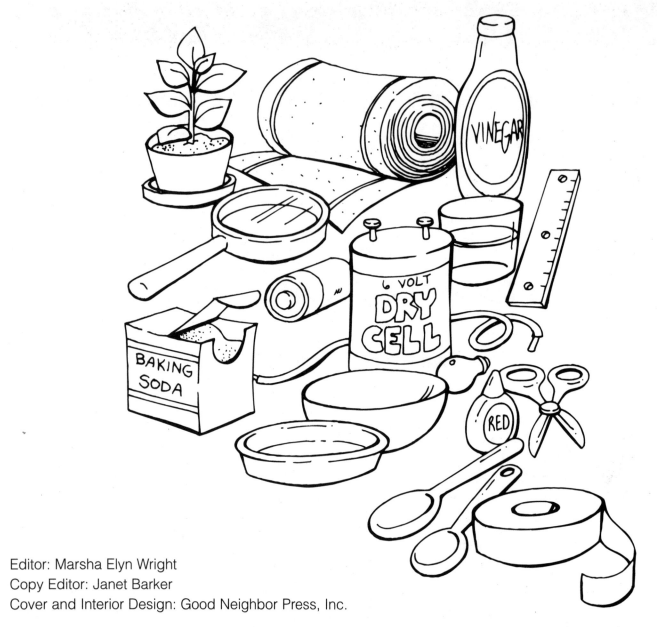

Editor: Marsha Elyn Wright
Copy Editor: Janet Barker
Cover and Interior Design: Good Neighbor Press, Inc.

Fearon Teacher Aids products were formerly manufactured and distributed by American Teaching Aids, Inc. a subsidiary of Silver Burdett Ginn, and are now manufactured and distributed by Frank Schaffer Publications, Inc. FEARON, FEARON TEACHER AIDS, and the FEARON balloon logo are marks used under license from Simon & Schuster, Inc.

FE11005

Fearon Teacher Aids

A Division of Frank Schaffer Publications, Inc.
23740 Hawthorne Boulevard
Torrance, CA 90505

© 1999 Fearon Teacher Aids. All rights reserved. Printed in the United States of America. This publication, or parts thereof, may not be reproduced in any form by photographic, electronic, mechanical, or any other method, for any use, including information storage and retrieval, without written permission from the publisher. Student reproducibles excepted.

Table of Contents

Teacher Tips for Science Centers iv
Class Record Chart 1

Plants/Soil
Leaf Print 2
How Plants Drink 3
A Tiny Terrarium 4
My Terrarium Record 5
Trapping Heat 6
My Temperature Record 7
Soil Shake 8
Moving Water 9
Leaves Help Soil 10
Leaf Shapes 11
Seeds with Two Parts 12
Seeds with One Part 13
Growing Seeds 14
My Seed Chart 15
Parts of a Plant 16

Animals
Animal Critter 17
My Animal Habitat 18

Water/Liquids
Bigger and Bigger 19
Sticky Water 20
My Water Chart 21
Rising Water 22
Changing Size 23
Water and Air Work Together 24
Changing Shape 25
Fun with Filters 26
My Filter Record 27
Sink or Float 28
My Sink and Float Chart 29
Lighter Than Water 30
Heavier Than Water 31
The Mix Up 32

Air/Water
Air Pushes 33
Air Is All Around Us 34
Air Slows Things Down 35
Touch Bottom 36
Water Insects 37
Round and Round 38
Spinning Wheels 39
Making a Siphon 40
My Siphon Record 41
Scrub-a-Dub Dub 42
Ice Cold 43

Sound
A Snappy Sound 44
Sound Travels 45
Sound Waves 46

Matter
The Blob 47

Color
Colorful Clay 48
My Color Wheel 49

Probability
A Good Chance 50
My Chance Record 51

Weights
Weighing In 52
My Weight Chart 53

Friction
Coasting Downhill 54

Simple Machines
Rolling Down a Ramp 55
Levers 56
My Lever Chart 57

Electricity
Let There Be Light 58
Stuck on You 59

Reproducible Awards
Awards: Super Scientist and Science Wizard 60

Teacher Tips for Science Centers

Fun with Science Centers provides 40 weeks worth of lessons to supplement your science curriculum or offers fun free-time activities. Each experiment can be done as a center activity with small groups, as a demonstration with the whole class, and as an independent activity for individual students. Each hands-on activity uses simple, inexpensive materials and equipment. Clear step-by-step instructions tell you how to easily construct any teacher-made items and how to prepare for each experiment. Each activity provides hands-on experience for children while teaching scientific principles and encouraging scientific curiosity.

Setting Up Science Centers is easy. Choose an area of the classroom away from other students to provide a quiet working environment. Ideally use a small table or a portion of a large table that has lots of space to store supplies and to perform the experiments. Set up enough chairs for each student if the class is working in small groups. Set up a new activity each week. Keep the center available all week. Rotate the students to work through the experiment as a class assignment, for extra credit, or as a special reward.

Student Record Sheets each contain a materials list, step-by-step directions, questions, a space for recording responses, and a section containing any needed information to prepare for the experiment and explanations and applications of the experiment. Reproduce this sheet for each student or enlarge it and display it at your center.

To provide an enriching follow-up, cover the teacher information at the bottom of the Record Sheet before reproducing it. After all of the students have completed the experiment, discuss as a class student results and any science concepts learned.

Use the Record Sheet as an answer key. Preread the experiment, perform it yourself, and fill in your own responses on a copy of the sheet. Post the answer key at the center for individuals or groups to check their own work. Or use the answer key on an overhead projector during a class discussion after everyone's completed the experiment.

For Younger Children read each experiment to determine which vocabulary and concepts need to be introduced and which experiments need to be demonstrated. There are several different ways to use the *Fun with Science Centers* for young learners:

- Work each experiment together as a class. Reproduce the Record Sheet for each student and have the children record their responses determined through class discussions. Demonstrate and do each experiment step-by-step for the students and request student helpers to assist you.

- Enlist the aid of parent volunteers to guide small groups of students through each experiment. First with the class, demonstrate the experiment, discuss the concepts, and introduce any difficult vocabulary. Then have small groups of children work with an adult to complete the experiment and record answers.

- Record the instructions for each experiment on a cassette tape and have the students replay the directions a few steps at a time while working in small groups or as individuals.

For Older Children use the experiments as extra-credit or enrichment activities. Put the children in "scientific teams" and challenge the students to see which team completes the most experiments during a trimester, a quarter, or the year! Give science-related rewards (hand lenses and animal information cards) to members of the winning team.

Center Rules can be posted to help the science center run smoothly:

- Read carefully.
- Follow directions.
- Work quietly.
- Work safely.
- Keep materials away from your eyes and mouth.
- Clean up.
- Print your name and the date on the Record Sheet.
- Turn in your Record Sheet.
- Follow the rules or lose your privilege of working at the Science Center!

Science Awards provided at the back of this book (page 60) can be given to each student upon completing an experiment. Let the children color and display their awards before sharing them with their families.

© Fearon Teacher Aids FE11005

Class Record Sheet for Science Centers

Student Names →

- Leaf Print
- How Plants Drink
- A Tiny Terrarium
- My Terrarium Record
- Trapping Heat
- My Temperature Record
- Soil Shake
- Moving Water
- Leaves Help Soil
- Leaf Shapes
- Seeds with Two Parts
- Seeds with One Part
- Growing Seeds
- My Seed Chart
- Parts of a Plant
- Animal Critter
- My Animal Habitat
- Bigger and Bigger
- Sticky Water
- My Water Chart
- Rising Water
- Changing Size
- Water and Air Work . . .
- Changing Shape
- Fun with Filters
- My Filter Record
- Sink or Float
- My Sink and Float Chart
- Lighter Than Water
- Heavier Than Water
- The Mix Up
- Air Pushes
- Air Is All Around Us
- Air Slows Things Down
- Touch Bottom
- Water Insects
- Round and Round
- Spinning Wheels
- Making a Siphon
- My Siphon Record
- Scrub-a-Dub Dub
- Ice Cold
- A Snappy Sound
- Sound Travels
- Sound Waves
- The Blob
- Colorful Clay
- My Color Wheel
- A Good Chance
- My Chance Record
- Weighing In
- My Weight Chart
- Coasting Downhill
- Rolling Down . . .
- Levers
- My Lever Chart
- Let There Be Light
- Stuck on You

© Fearon Teacher Aids FE11005

Reproducible

Record Sheet for _____ Date _____

Leaf Print

Materials:

marker
8½" x 11" sheet of wax paper
hand lens
pictures of different leaves
a leaf

Directions:

1. Hold the hand lens. Study your leaf.
   Mark a check by each word that tells about your leaf.

   ☐ big ☐ small ☐ long ☐ short ☐ round
   ☐ pointed ☐ wavy ☐ brittle ☐ soft ☐ thin

2. Move your fingers over the leaf. Look at the bumpy lines. These are called **veins**. Veins give the leaf its shape. They support the leaf.

3. Air gets into a leaf through tiny holes. Use your hand lens. Look for holes on your leaf.

4. Draw a picture of your leaf here.

5. Lay your leaf on wax paper. Use a marker to color the leaf. Place the leaf with the marker side down on the back of this paper. Press hard on the leaf. Do NOT slide your fingers. Lift up the leaf. There should be a leaf print.

Teacher: Before setting up this activity, take your students on a nature walk to collect leaves. Let each child collect one leaf. Display photographs and magazine and calendar pictures of leaves. After each student has completed a leaf print, talk with the class about leaves. Tell the children that the **veins** are tubes inside the leaf that carry food and water. The **stomata** are pores or holes that let in the carbon dioxide in the air and let out water vapor. Explain that the warming of the water in a leaf by the sun changes water into water vapor and is called **transpiration**. Use tree or leaf reference books such as May Theilgaard *Watts's Master Tree Finder* (Nature Study Guild, 1963) to help the children identify the names of their leaves and the trees from which their leaves grew.

Reproducible

© Fearon Teacher Aids FE11005

Record Sheet for _____ Date _____

How Plants Drink

Materials:

water
food coloring
two 6-inch squares of paper towel
two clear plastic cups
tape

Directions:

1. Fill each cup half full of water.
2. Add two drops of food coloring to one cup.
3. Roll each square of paper towel into a tube shape. Tape.
4. Place one tube in each cup. Watch closely!
5. Draw what happens in each cup.

Clear Water

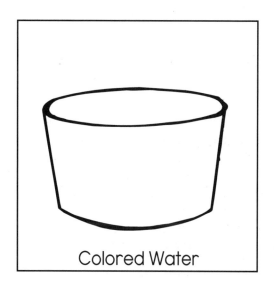
Colored Water

6. Does the colored water move up faster than the clear water? _____
7. Will the water go to the top of each tube? _____

Teacher: Tell the children that the paper tubes are similar to the **stems** of plants. The water moves through the holes in the paper just like water moves through the **stomata** in leaves. The clear water and the colored water should move up the paper towel at the same rate although the colored water is easier to see. Tell the children that water carries food (**nutrients**) and other substances to the leaves.

Record Sheet for _____ Date _____

A Tiny Terrarium

Materials:

water
clean, wide-mouthed glass jar with lid
small gravel
potting soil
plant cutting
ruler

Directions:

1. Put gravel in the bottom of the jar.

2. Cover the gravel with soil. Leave air space so your plant can grow.

3. Poke your finger into the soil. Put your plant in the hole. Press the soil around the plant.

4. Water your plant. Screw on the lid. Place the jar near a window.

5. Each day check your terrarium. If it looks foggy, take off the lid. When it clears, replace the lid.

6. Draw how your terrarium looks each day for five days. Use My Terrarium Record sheet.

Teacher: To prepare for this experiment, show the children how to put just a one-inch layer of gravel inside their jars and how to cover it with about three inches of soil. Show them how to gently poke a hole in the soil for their plants. Tell the children that a **terrarium** is a mini-closed-up environment. Air and moisture are trapped around the plant. When the sun shines on a terrarium, heat is also trapped inside the jar. Water is cycled within the terrarium. Heat causes the water to **evaporate**, or change into water vapor, but it cannot escape. Water also **transpires**, or comes out of the plant through the leaves as water vapor. This water is also trapped. Since the water vapor cannot escape, it condenses, or turns back into water, and sticks to the inside of the jar. If the terrarium gets too hot or is in direct sunlight for a long time, the jar will get foggy. It gets foggy because the water has turned to water vapor and has condensed faster than the plants and soil can absorb it. To remove fog, open the lid for about an hour until it clears. You can also move the jars a little farther from the sunshine. You don't need to keep watering the terrariums as long as the lids are in place. Each child should water his or her terrarium with only ¼ cup of water. The closed jars will preserve the temperature and the moisture. If there seems to be too much moisture in a jar, open the lid to let some evaporate. If a terrarium stays too wet, mold will grow, the roots will rot, and the plant will suffer. Reproduce page 5 for each student. Have the students record their observations on this record sheet.

Reproducible © Fearon Teacher Aids FE11005

Name _____ Date _____

Observation Recording

My Terrarium Record

Draw how your terrarium looks each day.

Day One	Day Two	Day Three

Day Four	Day Five

TEACHER: Reproduce this record sheet for each student. Use it with the experiment A Tiny Terrarium on page 4. (You may want the children to write in the date for each day.)

© Fearon Teacher Aids FE11005 — Reproducible

Record Sheet for _____ Date _____

Trapping Heat

Materials:

two thermometers
string or twist ties
wire coat hanger
plastic bag with a twist tie

Directions:

1. Use twist ties to hang a thermometer at each end of a coat hanger.

2. Hang the hanger in a sunny window. Try to have both thermometers show the same temperature. Look at each thermometer. Record the temperatures on My Temperature Record.

3. Slide a plastic bag over one thermometer. Use a twist tie to shut the bag and keep it in place.

4. Hang the hanger in the sun again for about 15 minutes.

5. Read the temperatures on both thermometers. Record the temperatures on My Temperature Record.

6. Which temperature is higher—the one with the bag or without the bag?

_____

7. Why do you think one temperature is higher than the other?

_____

Teacher: Reproduce My Temperature Record on page 7 for each student. After the children have completed this experiment, tell them that the plastic bag kept the air trapped around the one thermometer so it couldn't move. The air got hotter and hotter so the temperature rose fast. The heat was trapped and could not escape very quickly in the sun. This is similar to the concept that happens in a greenhouse. It is also like the concept that keeps Earth warm. There is a layer of air around Earth called the **atmosphere**. The sun shines on the earth and heats up everything. Our atmosphere traps some of this heat and insulates the earth.

Name _____   Date _____

My Temperature Record

Observation Recording

Fill in each thermometer to show the temperature readings. Write the degrees.

Temperatures After 15 Minutes

Without the Bag

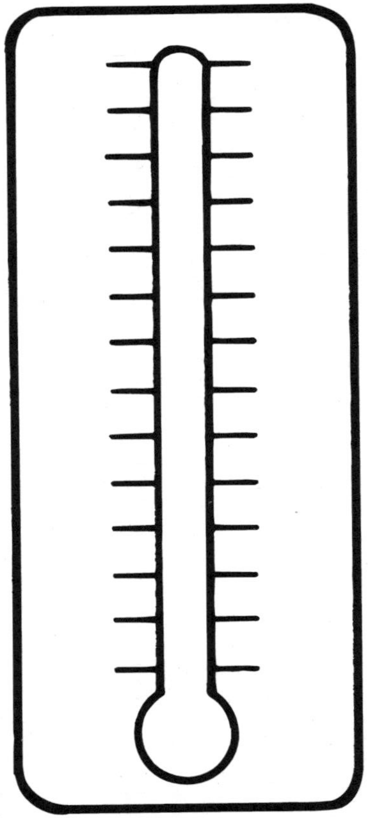

_____ degrees

With the Bag

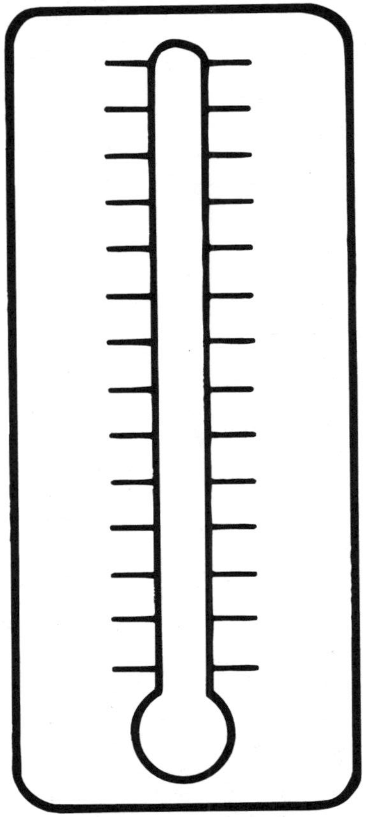

_____ degrees

Starting Temperatures

Without the Bag

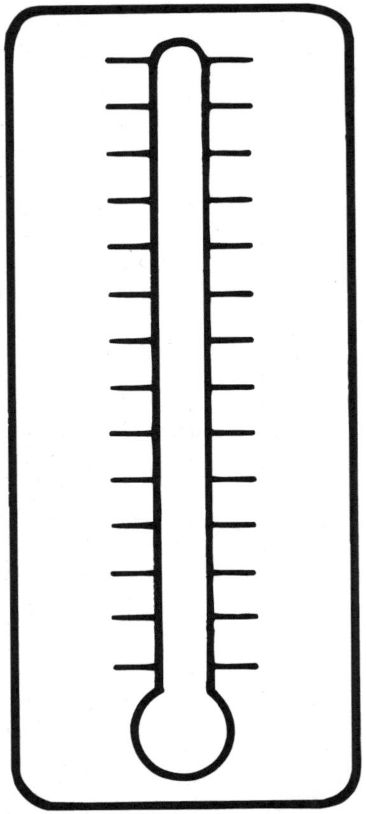

_____ degrees

With the Bag

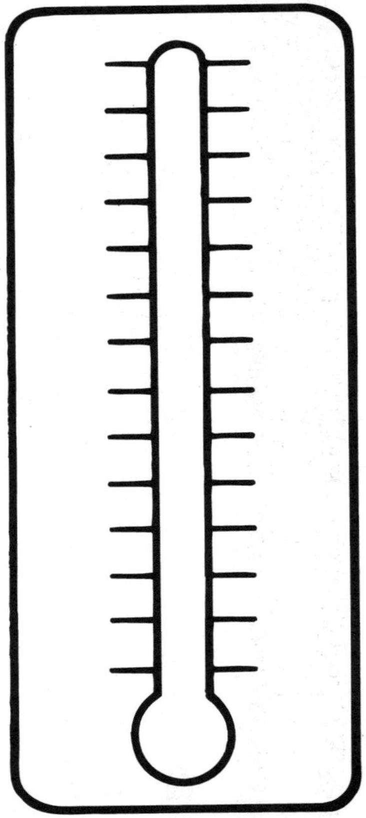

_____ degrees

Teacher: Reproduce this record sheet for each student. Use it with the experiment Trapping Heat on page 6. Have the children use a red crayon to fill in each thermometer.

© Fearon Teacher Aids FE11005

Reproducible

Record Sheet for _____ Date _____

Soil Shake

Materials:

water
soil with small rocks
teaspoon
two clean, empty baby food jars with lids
hand lens
trash can
piece of scrap paper

Directions:

1. Put some soil on the paper. Look at it through a hand lens. List what you see.

   _____

2. Put a few spoonfuls of soil in each jar.

3. Pour water in one jar. Screw on the lid. Shake the jar over a trash can. Then set it on a table next to the other jar.

4. Draw a picture of how each jar looks right now.

Jar with Water

Jar without Water

5. Wait a few minutes. Look at the jars again. On the back of this paper, draw what the inside of each jar looks like.

Teacher: After the children have completed this experiment, talk with them about what happens. The dry soil doesn't rearrange itself. The wet soil rearranges itself because it is shaken in water and the things in the soil have different levels of **buoyancy**. Buoyancy means how well something can float. The jar with the water should look like a layer cake—the heaviest things (like rocks) settles to the bottom first. Heavier soil settles next, followed by the lightest soil. Some bits of matter may be light enough to remain floating.

Reproducible © Fearon Teacher Aids FE11005

Record Sheet for _____ Date _____

Moving Water

Materials:

clean peanut butter jar
sand
small pebbles
teaspoon
water

Directions:

1. Put the sand and pebbles on the bottom of the jar. Make a thin layer.

2. Pour water in the jar so it is almost full. Write what happens.

   _____
   _____

3. Wait a few minutes. Write any changes you see.

   _____
   _____

4. Stir the water slowly. Do NOT touch the sand and rocks. Now stir faster. Write what happens.

   _____
   _____
   _____

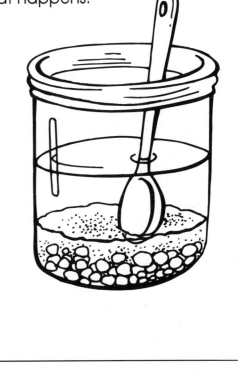

5. Watch the jar. What settles to the bottom first? _____

6. What settles to the bottom last? _____

7. Does anything float? _____

Teacher: Tell the students that they are simulating what happens in a river. Rivers carry along soil, rocks, and sand as they flow. At points along the river, the water slows down and some or all of the moving materials settle at the bottom. These materials are called **sediment**. The more sediment that is dropped by the river in one place the more the water is slowed in that place. The build-up of sediment forms sandbars and small islands in the river. At the end or mouth of the river, the sediment build-up is called a **delta**.

© Fearon Teacher Aids FE11005   Reproducible

Record Sheet for _____ Date _____

Leaves Help Soil

Materials:

water in small plastic pitcher
sand
brick
pie pan
scissors
three paper leaves
tin can with holes poked in bottom

Directions:

1. Cut out the leaves on the Leaf Shapes sheet.

2. Place the brick in the pan. Cover the top of the brick with sand. Lay each leaf on top of the sand.

3. Make it "rain" on the sand. Hold the can over the brick. Slowly pour water into the can. Watch the water drain down and flow through the holes.

4. Look at the sand now. Write how it looks.

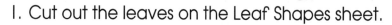
_____

5. Lift up each leaf. Look at the sand under it. What do you see?

6. Leaves help keep soil from being washed away by rain. What other things in nature protect the soil this way? Write their names.

_____

Teacher: To prepare for this experiment, reproduce the leaf shapes on page 11 on tagboard or heavy green construction paper. Make one set of leaves for each student. You can also use page 10 to make tagboard leaf patterns and have each student trace and color their leaves. Use a nail to punch 20 to 30 small holes in the bottom of a tin can. After the students have completed this experiment, talk with them about how leaves protect the soil. They keep the soil from being washed away by rain, rivers, lakes, melting snow, and oceans. Other natural protectors of the soil are grass, sticks, logs, moss, living and nonliving plants, and decaying trees.

Name _____ Date _____

Experimenting

Leaf Shapes

Cut out the leaves.

Teacher: Reproduce this page on tagboard or heavy green construction paper for each student. Let the students use the leaves to do the experiment Leaves Help Soil on page 10.

© Fearon Teacher Aids FE11005   Reproducible

Record Sheet for _____ Date _____

Seeds with Two Parts

Materials:

water in small margarine tub
dried bean seeds
sheet of paper towel
hand lens

Directions:

1. Soak one seed in the water. Lay the other seed on the paper towel. Draw a picture of each seed.

2. Study the seeds. Which seed looks bigger?

Wet Seed	Dry Seed

_____

3. Pick up each seed. Mark a check by each word that tells how it feels.

Wet Seed: ☐ wet ☐ slippery ☐ slimy ☐ hard ☐ soft ☐ cold

Dry Seed: ☐ dry ☐ smooth ☐ bumpy ☐ hard ☐ soft ☐ warm

4. Pick up the dry seed. Try to peel off its skin. The skin is called the **seed coat**.

   Is it **easy** or **hard** to peel off its seed coat? _____

5. Pick up the wet seed. Try to peel off its seed coat. Is it **easy** or **hard** to peel off?

_____

6. Open each seed. How many pieces did you find? _____

7. Use a hand lens. Study your seeds. Draw a picture of each seed.

Wet Seed	Dry Seed

Teacher: For this experiment, use pinto or lima beans. For the wet seeds, let the students soak their seeds for at least 20 minutes. Tell the students that seeds with two halves are called **dicots**. All pinto beans and lima beans as well as many other beans are dicots. The seed halves are filled with the first food needed by the beginnings of the young plant in the seed.

Record Sheet for _____ Date _____

Seeds with One Part

Materials:

water in small margarine tub
dried corn seeds
sheet of paper towel
hand lens

Directions:

1. Soak one seed in the water. Lay the other seed on the paper towel. Draw a picture of each seed.

2. Study the seeds. Which seed looks bigger?
   _____

Wet Seed	Dry Seed

3. Pick up each seed. Mark a check by each word that tells how it feels.

   Wet Seed: ☐ wet ☐ slippery ☐ slimy ☐ hard ☐ soft ☐ cold

   Dry Seed: ☐ dry ☐ smooth ☐ bumpy ☐ hard ☐ soft ☐ warm

4. Pick up the dry seed. Try to peel off its skin. The skin is called the **seed coat**.

   Is it **easy** or **hard** to peel off its seed coat? _____

5. Pick up the wet seed. Try to peel off its seed coat. Is it **easy** or **hard** to peel off?
   _____

6. Open each seed. How many pieces did you find? _____

7. Use a hand lens. Study your seeds. Draw a picture of each seed.

Wet Seed	Dry Seed

Teacher: For this experiment, use corn seeds. For the wet seeds, let the students soak their seeds for at least 20 minutes. Tell the students that seeds made up of one part are called **monocots**. All corn seeds as well as many other seeds are monocots. Even though there is only one part, it is still full of the first food needed by the beginnings of the young plant in the seed.

Record Sheet for _____ Date _____

Growing Seeds

Materials:

- clear plastic cup
- black construction paper
- three lima bean seeds
- potting soil
- tablespoon
- masking tape
- rubber band
- scissors
- pencil

Directions:

1. Fill the cup almost full with soil.

2. Use a pencil to poke three holes in the soil. Make the holes close to the edge of the cup. Place one seed in each hole.

3. Press the soil over each seed. You should still see the seeds through the side of the cup.

4. Stick a piece of tape on the side of the cup by each seed. Do NOT hide the seeds.

5. Label each seed on the pieces of tape. Print **A**, **B**, and **C**.

6. Cut a piece of black paper to fit around the cup. Wrap it around the cup. Put a rubber band over the paper to hold it in place.

7. Water each seed.

8. Follow the directions on My Seed Chart.

Teacher: Reproduce My Seed Chart and Parts of a Plant (pages 15 and 16) for each student. Help the students cut the black construction paper to fit around their cups. Read and discuss the instructions on My Seed Chart so the students understand what to do each day. (This activity will take about five days.) Tell the students that when they water their seeds, they should use about two tablespoons of water for each seed. Discuss with your students what they are observing each day—the growth and development of a seed into a young plant. Let the children take home their plants after the experiment. Display the plant pictures.

Name _____ Date _____

Observation Recording

My Seed Chart

Take off the black paper. Look at the seeds. Draw how each seed looks.

	Day 1	Day 2	Day 3	Day 4	Day 5
Seed A 					
Seed B 					
Seed C 					

Teacher: Reproduce this page and page 16 for each student. Use the pages with the experiment Growing Seeds on page 14. Let the children observe their seeds for five days.

© Fearon Teacher Aids FE11005

Reproducible

Record Sheet for _____ Date _____

Parts of a Plant

Science, Identification

Plants make the food we eat and the oxygen we breathe. Cut out the labels and glue them to name the plant parts.

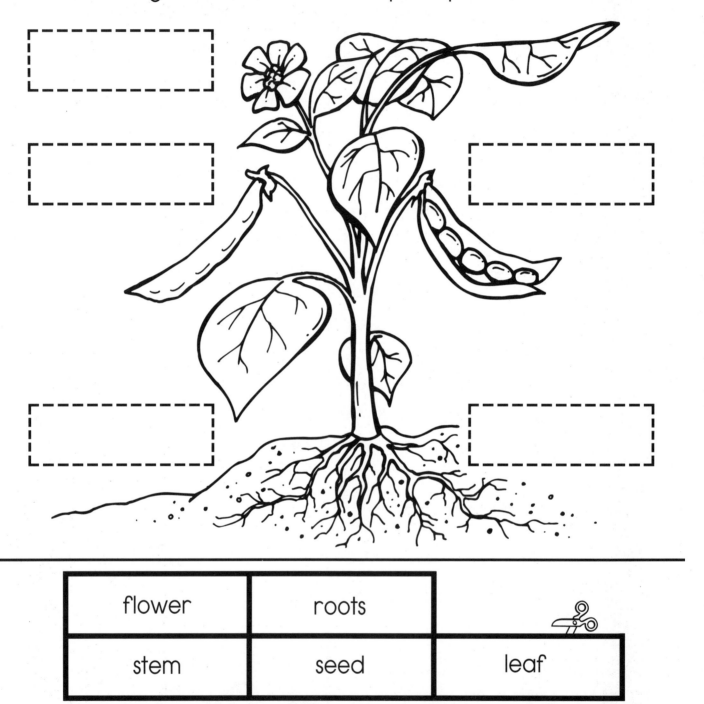

flower	roots	
stem	seed	leaf

Teacher: Reproduce this page and pages 14 and 15 for each student. Let the students use them to do the experiment Growing Plants (page 14). Discuss how important plants are to life on earth. Plants produce the **oxygen** we breathe and the food we eat. Let the students cut out the labels, glue them in their correct locations to identify the plant parts, and color the plants. Let them draw their own pictures of plants. Display their plant part diagrams and their pictures for all to enjoy!

Record Sheet for _____ Date _____

Animal Critter

Materials:

clay   crayons
straws   scissors
toothpicks   pencil

Directions:

1. Make an animal out of clay, toothpicks, and straws. It can be a real animal or a make-believe one.

2. Look at your animal. It should have a body part for getting food. It should have parts to help it move.

3. Draw a picture of your animal.

4. Think about your animal. Fill in the card below. Cut it out.

My Animal

Name _____

My Animal

The name of my animal is _____.

It lives in the _____.

It eats _____.

It moves by _____.

It is special because it _____
_____
_____.

Teacher: Reproduce My Animal Habitat on page 18 for each student and use it with this activity. After each student makes an animal habitat, have the student tape the animal card from this page on the animal habitat.

Name _____ Date _____

Animal habitats

My Animal Habitat

TAB		TAB
TAB		TAB

1. Color your animal habitat.
2. Draw its home.
3. Draw its food.
4. Cut on the ———— lines.
5. Fold on the ·········· lines.
6. Glue the TABS to make a box.

Teacher: Reproduce this page on tagboard or heavy light blue construction paper for each student. Demonstrate to the children how to fold on the dotted lines and cut on the solid lines to make a box habitat. Talk with your students about where animals live—ponds, mountains, deserts, grasslands, prairies, forests, jungles, etc. Tell the students that where an animal lives is called its **habitat**. After the students complete their animal habitats, display the animals, the animal cards, and habitats on a counter or table for all to enjoy.

Reproducible

18

© Fearon Teacher Aids FE11005

Record Sheet for _____ Date _____

Bigger and Bigger

Materials:

newspaper
eye dropper
pencil
water
clear plastic cup
clear sheet of plastic wrap

Directions:

1. Lay the plastic on the newspaper. Use an eye dropper. Put a few drops of water together on the plastic.

2. Find a letter in the newspaper. Write it. _____

3. Now look through the big water drop. Try to read a letter in the newspaper. Write it. _____

4. Which letter looks bigger—the letter you see **through the plastic** or the letter you see **through the water**?

   _____

5. Pour some water in a cup. Hold a pencil behind the cup.

6. Look through the water. How does the pencil look? Can you read words on it? Draw what you see.

7. Put the pencil inside the cup. Look at the pencil through the water again. Does one part look bigger? Draw what you see.

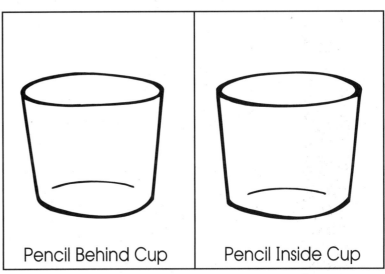

Pencil Behind Cup | Pencil Inside Cup

Teacher: Tell the students that when an object is close to the cup of water, the water in the cup acts like a hand lens and **magnifies** the object (makes it look larger than it is). Water can magnify objects even if it is not in a container. When the students looked through the water drop at the newspaper, the letters looked larger. Not only the water, but the shape of the water helps to magnify things.

© Fearon Teacher Aids FE11005 — Reproducible

Record Sheet for _____   Date _____

Sticky Water

Materials:

penny, nickel, and dime
clean water
soapy water
eye dropper
paper towels

Directions:

1. Place a penny heads up on a paper towel.

2. Use an eye dropper. Put one drop of clean water on top of the penny. The water "sticks to itself." It stays on the penny!

3. How many drops will stay on the penny? Write your guess on My Water Chart.

4. Count each drop as you put it on the penny. STOP when the water spills off.

5. Record the drops you put on the penny. Write the number on My Water Chart.

6. Repeat this activity for the dime and the nickel.

7. Now guess how many drops of soapy water will stay on the penny, the nickel, and the dime. Write your guesses on My Water Chart.

8. Use the eye dropper again. Take one coin at a time. Put a drop of soapy water on it.

9. Count each drop. STOP when the water spills.

10. Record the drops. Write the number on My Water Chart.

Teacher: For this experiment, have a container of clean, tap water and a container of water with liquid detergent in it. Reproduce My Water Chart on page 21 for each student. Help your students see how water is a liquid that seems to flow, and yet it sticks to itself. The **molecules** pull together (**surface tension**). Tell the students that the next time they look at a dripping water faucet to look closely and see how the water seems to "hang" as if it doesn't want to let go before it drops. When the droplet does drop, it quickly changes in a "ball shape." Surface tension causes this. Tell the students that surface tension in water can be good, especially for insects that walk on water. But it can cause problems when we try to clean things. Soap and detergent reduce the surface tension. That's why it's important to use soap when cleaning our hands and clothes. That's why fewer drops were able to stick together on the soapy coins.

Reproducible   © Fearon Teacher Aids FE11005

Name _____ Date _____

Observation Recording

My Water Chart

Coins	Clean Water		Soapy Water	
	Guess	Drops	Guess	Drops
 penny				
 dime				
 nickel				

Teacher: Reproduce this page for each student. Use it with the experiment Sticky Water on page 20. Let the children share their results with the class.

© Fearon Teacher Aids FE11005

Reproducible

Record Sheet for _____ Date _____

Rising Water

Materials:

water
sheet of paper
eye dropper
two small pieces of wax paper

Directions:

1. Use an eye dropper. Put a drop of water on each piece of wax paper. Separate the pieces.

2. Fold a sheet of paper back and forth to make a fan. Fan one drop of water.

3. Watch the water drops. When water gets warm, it changes into a gas. The gas rises into the air.

4. Which drop changed first—the **fanned drop** or the **drop left alone**? Make an **X** to show your answer on the chart.

5. Do this activity two more times. Share what you learned.

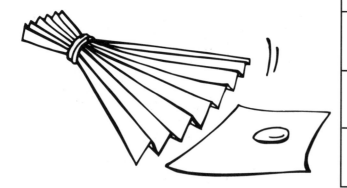

Tries	Fanned Water Drop	Water Drop Left Alone
#1 Try		
#2 Try		
#3 Try		

Teacher: For this experiment, have a container of clean, tap water. Show the students how to fold a sheet of white paper back and forth to make a fan. Tell the students that when water gets warm it doesn't just dry up; it changes form. It changes from a liquid into a gas (**water vapor**). Water is always changing into water vapor. Both drops will evaporate (change into water vapor), however, the fanned drop of water should evaporate first. Moving air and heat together or by themselves can help speed up the change. Some evaporated water rises high into the sky, sticking to smoke and dust and forming clouds. The water vapor eventually falls back to earth as **precipitation** (rain, sleet, hail, or snow).

Reproducible   © Fearon Teacher Aids FE11005

Record Sheet for _____ Date _____

Changing Size

Materials:

cup marked **A**
cup marked **B**
two clean plastic cups
teaspoon
eye dropper
sheet of wax paper
sheet of white paper
water

Directions:

1. Put a spoonful of **Cup A** on the wax paper.

2. Put a spoonful of **Cup B** on the wax paper.

3. Feel the two piles. Taste them. Which cup has sugar? Which cup has salt?

   Cup A has _____. **Cup B** has _____.

4. Pour water into the clean cups. Stir sugar into the **Sugar** cup. Stir salt into the **Salt** cup. Watch the moving water in each cup.

6. Do the salt and sugar **change in the water** or do they **stay on the bottom**?

   The salt and sugar

   _____.

7. Fold a sheet of paper to make a fan. Put a drop of water from each cup on wax paper. Fan each drop.

8. Taste each pile left on the wax paper.

   Do you taste the sugar and salt? _____

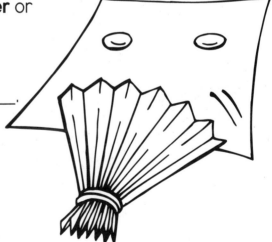

Teacher: For this experiment, have a cup of sugar marked **A** and one of salt marked **B**. Label with tape one of the clean plastic cups *SALT* and the other one *SUGAR*. Put water in a pitcher that's easy to pour. Remind the students to wash their hands. Show the students how to fold a sheet of paper to make a fan. Tell the students that sugar and salt are made up of tiny bits called **molecules**. When the sugar and salt are put into the water, the molecules separate into smaller bits (**dissolve**). The molecules change size. When the water evaporates into the air, it can't carry the dissolved sugar and salt with it so the sugar and salt remain on the wax paper.

© Fearon Teacher Aids FE11005   Reproducible

Record Sheet for _____ Date _____

Water and Air Work Together

Materials:

small drinking glass
water
trash can
4" x 6" sturdy index card (or cardboard)

Directions:

1. Lay an index card over the opening of a glass. Press your hand firmly on top of the index card to hold it in place.

2. Keep pressing on the card and completely turn over the glass and card.

3. Slowly remove your hand from the card. Does the card **fall** or **stay in place**?

   I saw the card _____.

4. Fill the glass with water. Put the card on the opening again. Hold it firmly in place.

5. Hold the glass over a trash can. Keep pressing on the card and completely turn over the glass and card.

6. Slowly remove your hand from the card.

   Does the card **fall** or **stay in place**?

   I saw the card _____.

7. Turn the glass and card right side up. Remove the card.

Teacher: This is a difficult experiment to do successfully. Demonstrate to the students how to firmly hold an index card on top of a glass so that there is no air space anywhere between the card and the opening of the glass. Show them how to hold onto the glass with the other hand. Demonstrate how to hang on firmly to everything and with one motion turn the whole thing completely upside down. When the students try this with water in the glass, have them do the experiment over a trash can in case something slips and the water spills out. Tell your students that water creates an airtight seal with the card. **Air pressure** under the card of the water-filled glass is pushing up harder on the card than the water is pushing down on the card. Pulling down on one edge of the card or inserting a pencil between the index card and the glass would break the airtight seal. If the airtight seal is broken, air pushes in and the water falls out!

Reproducible   © Fearon Teacher Aids FE11005

Record Sheet for _____ Date _____

Changing Shape

Materials:

ball of clay
masking tape
marker
wide-mouthed jar
water

1
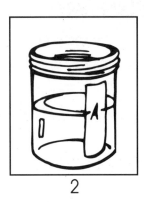
2

Directions:

1. Pour water in the jar. See picture 1.

2. Put a long strip of tape up and down on the jar. See picture 2.

3. Mark a line where the water is. Make an **A** by this line. See picture 2.

4. Put the clay into the jar. Did the water **go above the line** or **stay the same**?

   I saw the water _____.

5. Mark a line where the water is now. Make a **B** by this line. See picture 3.

6. Take out the clay. Did the water **stay above the line** or **go down to meet the line**?

   I saw the water _____.

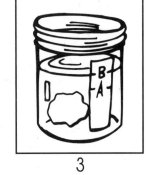
3

7. Change the shape of the clay. Draw a picture of it on the back of this paper.

8. Put your clay shape into the jar. Did the water **meet line A** or **meet line B**?

   I saw the water _____.

Teacher: Demonstrate to the students how to mark their tape lines **A** and **B**. When the students change the shape of their clay, tell them not to add or take away from their amount of clay. They are just to change the shape. The students can also break their clay into pieces and place the pieces in the water. Tell students that the water level was always the same, even when they added the clay. The volume of the clay remains the same, only the shape is changed. We can change the shape of something, make it into pieces, or put the pieces together, but the amount of clay will stay the same. Nothing in nature is lost. There is always the same amount of stuff (**matter**). Matter just changes shape, size, the number of pieces, and how it looks. Sometimes matter mixes with other matter to make totally new kinds of things, and sometimes matter separates into its different kinds of pieces (**elements**). But the amount of matter stays the same.

Record Sheet for _____ Date _____

Fun with Filters

Materials:

sugar water
sandy water
half-pint empty milk carton (with top cut off)
clean peanut butter jar
nail
two paper towels

Directions:

1. Punch six nail holes in the bottom of the carton.

2. Place one paper towel inside the carton.

3. Place the carton on top of the jar to make a **filter**.

   A **filter** is something that lets liquid flow through it and stops most solid things from flowing through it.

4. Slowly pour sandy water into the filter. Record what you see happen on My Filter Record.

5. Take out the wet, sandy paper towel. Lay another paper towel inside the carton.

6. Slowly pour sugar water into the filter. Record what you see happen on My Filter Record.

7. What did you learn? (Circle) the correct sentence.

   The filter stopped ALL of the solid things mixed with the liquid.

   The filter stopped only the BIG solid things mixed with the liquid.

Teacher: To prepare for this experiment, add two tablespoons of sugar to one cup of water to make sugar water. Add two tablespoons of sand to one cup of water. Mix each liquid well. Put each into an easy-to-pour container (two-cup measuring cup). Cut the top off of a half-pint milk carton. Help the students use nails to poke about six holes in the bottom of their milk cartons. Remind the students about using nails safely so they don't get poked. Reproduce My Filter Record page 27 for each student. Read the questions and possible answers together. Have the students record their observations by circling the words. Tell the children that a **filter** is any device through which a liquid passes to be strained. The filter lets the liquid through and stops most solid materials. How much of the solid gets through depends on these things: (1) the size of the holes or spaces in the filter and (2) the size of the solid. The sand was too large to fit through the spaces in the paper towel fibers. After the sugar dissolved, it was small enough to fit through the spaces.

Reproducible   © Fearon Teacher Aids FE11005

Name _____ Date _____

My Filter Record

Observation Recording

Read each question. Circle your answer.

Sandy Water

1. What went through the filter?   sand   water
2. What was it?   solid   liquid   gas
3. What did not go through the filter?   sand   water
4. What was it?   solid   liquid   gas

Sugar Water

1. Do both the sugar and the water go through the filter?   yes   no
2. What is sugar **before** it is mixed with water?   solid   liquid   gas
3. What does sugar become like **after it is mixed** with water?   solid   liquid   gas

Teacher: Reproduce this page for each student. Read the questions and possible answers together as a class. Use this page with the experiment Fun with Filters on page 26.

© Fearon Teacher Aids FE11005

27

Reproducible

Record Sheet for _____ Date _____

Sink or Float

Materials:

bowl of water
towel
objects to test

Directions:

1. Line up each object.

2. Guess if it will **sink** or **float** in the water. Record your guess on My Sink and Float Chart.

3. Place the object on the water. Does it **sink** or **float**? Record what happens on My Sink and Float Chart.

4. Did you guess correctly? Record your answer on My Sink and Float Chart.

5. Repeat this activity for each object.

6. Draw a picture of three objects that **float** and three objects that **sink**.

Objects that Float	Objects that Sink

Teacher: To prepare for this experiment, pour water into a clear, glass bowl so it's about three-fourths full. Gather objects that the students can test whether they sink or float—pencil, peanut in its shell, crayon, paper clip, rock, nail, comb, toothpick, craft stick, pingpong ball, jacks ball, clothes pin, bar of Ivory™ soap, safety pin, marble, apple, Styrofoam™ cup. Write the names of the objects you want the students to test on My Sink and Float Chart page 29. Then reproduce the chart for each student. After the students experiment, tell them that **buoyancy** is the ability of a liquid to keep an object floating. The size, shape, and weight of an object will affect the water's ability to keep it floating. Buoyancy is also affected by the amount of water in which the object floats or sinks. Some materials such as cork and Styrofoam™ almost always float in water no matter what.

Reproducible   **28**   © Fearon Teacher Aids FE11005

Name _____ Date _____

Sink and Float Chart

(Circle) your answers.

Object	Your Guess	What it Did	Were You Right?
	float sink	float sink	Yes No
	float sink	float sink	Yes No
	float sink	float sink	Yes No
	float sink	float sink	Yes No
	float sink	float sink	Yes No
	float sink	float sink	Yes No
	float sink	float sink	Yes No
	float sink	float sink	Yes No
	float sink	float sink	Yes No
	float sink	float sink	Yes No
	float sink	float sink	Yes No

Observation Recording

Name _____   Date _____

Sink and Float Chart

Observation Recording

Circle your answers.

Object	Your Guess	What it Did	Were You Right?
	float sink	float sink	Yes No
	float sink	float sink	Yes No
	float sink	float sink	Yes No
	float sink	float sink	Yes No
	float sink	float sink	Yes No
	float sink	float sink	Yes No
	float sink	float sink	Yes No
	float sink	float sink	Yes No
	float sink	float sink	Yes No
	float sink	float sink	Yes No

Teacher: Use this page with the experiment Sink or Float on page 28. Write in each object that the students will test, then reproduce the record sheet for each student.

© Fearon Teacher Aids FE11005

Reproducible

Record Sheet for _____ Date _____

Lighter Than Water

Materials:

12-inch square of aluminum foil
paper clips
wax paper
wide pan with water

Directions:

1. Shape your foil into a boat. Test to see if it floats. If it doesn't, shape it again.

2. Draw a picture of your boat.

3. Add one paper clip at a time in the boat until it sinks. How many paper clips did your boat hold before it sank?

   _____

4. Make a new boat shape to see if it will hold more paper clips. Test the boat to see if it floats. Draw your new boat.

5. Float your new boat. Add one paper clip at a time in the boat until it sinks.

6. How many paper clips did your boat hold before it sank? _____

7. Crumple the foil boat into a ball. Does it **float** or **sink**? _____

8. Smash the foil ball flat. Push out all the air. Does it **float** or **sink**? _____

Boat #1

Boat #2

Teacher: To prepare for this experiment, pour water into a dishpan or other wide container. Have a towel on hand for water spills. Tell the children that aluminum foil is very light. A sheet of foil easily floats until it is covered or filled with water or other objects. The children's boats should hold at least several paper clips. As more weight is added to the boat, its buoyancy is reduced. The ball of aluminum floats because the spaces between the crumples are full of air. When the ball is smashed, the air is pushed out. The smashed ball sinks because there is just a little air trapped inside of it. To vary the experiment, as a class try making boats and seeing how many pennies float on them before they sink or put your students in small groups and see which group's boat holds the most pennies!

Record Sheet for _____ Date _____

Heavier Than Water

Materials:

ball of clay
paper clips
wax paper
wide pan with water

Directions:

1. Put your clay on the wax paper. Shape your clay into a boat. Test to see if it floats. If it doesn't, shape it again.

2. Draw a picture of your boat.

3. Add one paper clip at a time in the boat until it sinks. How many paper clips did your boat hold before it sank?

   _____

4. Make a new boat shape to see if it will hold more paper clips. Test the boat to see if it floats. Draw your new boat.

5. Float your new boat. Add one paper clip at a time in the boat until it sinks.

6. How many paper clips did your boat hold before it sank? _____

7. Roll your clay boat into a ball. Does it **float** or **sink**? _____

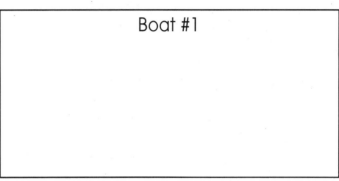

Boat #1

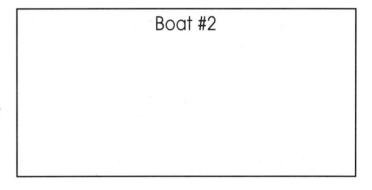

Boat #2

Teacher: To prepare for this experiment, pour water into a wide container. Have a towel on hand for water spills. Tell the children that clay is heavier than water. If left in a ball the clay sinks. The shape of the clay affects whether or not it will float. When the clay is spread out thin and has raised sides, the clay displaces more water which enables it to float. Since air is lighter than water, the clay boat floats. But the more paper clips added to the boat, the more the boat weighs and the less space there is for air. So the heavy boat sinks. Ships today are partly made of steel. Steel is heavier than water. These ships must be built hollow to capture air. The air inside is lighter than water and helps the ship float. When we talk about how well something floats, we call this its **buoyancy**. To vary the experiment, as a class try making boats and seeing how many pennies float on them before they sink.

Record Sheet for _____ Date _____

The Mix Up

Materials:

clear plastic cup
bowl
teaspoon
food coloring
baking soda
vinegar in a cup

Directions:

1. Place the cup in the bowl. Put a spoonful of baking soda in the cup.
2. Add a few drops of food coloring to the vinegar.
3. Pour the vinegar mixture into the cup with the soda. Watch what happens.
4. (Circle) the true sentence. Draw a picture to show it.

   The soda and vinegar forms a gas that makes bubbles.

   The soda and vinegar forms a mixture that doesn't make a gas.

```
┌─────────────────────────────────────────────────────────────┐
│                                                             │
│                                                             │
│                                                             │
│                                                             │
│                                                             │
│                                                             │
│   Right after mixing the vinegar, food coloring, and baking soda. │
└─────────────────────────────────────────────────────────────┘
```

Teacher: Tell the children that sometimes different substances combine to make a new substance. In this experiment, a **gas** forms by mixing the vinegar and the baking soda. This gas produces the bubbles. The food coloring makes the bubbles change color.

Reproducible   **32**   © Fearon Teacher Aids FE11005

Record Sheet for _____ Date _____

Air Pushes

Materials:

heavy book
lunch bag

Directions:

1. Open the lunch bag. Blow into it. What happens to the bag?

   The bag _____ .
           gets bigger   stays flat

2. Why does this happen?

   The bag _____ .
          loses its air   fills with air

3. Place the bag on a desk or table. Have the open end go out over the edge.

4. Stand a book up on the bag.

5. Put your finger in the bag. Bunch the end of the bag around your finger.

6. Remove your finger and blow into the bag. What happens to the book?

   The book _____ .
          falls over   stays standing

7. Why does this happen? (Circle) the true sentence.

   The force of the air going into the bag pushes the book over.

   The bag stays empty but it knocks the book over anyway.

Teacher: Tell the children that air has a force, or pressure. **Air pressure** is always around us and is always trying to create the same amount of pressure inside and outside of things. Although air itself cannot be seen, we can experience its presence and effects all the time. Air takes up space and can lift things. The pressure of the air being forced into the bag pushes over the book.

Record Sheet for _____ Date _____

Air Is All Around Us

Materials:

plastic cup of water
food coloring
straw

Directions:

1. Add two drops of food coloring to the water.

2. Stir it with the straw.

3. Hold the straw above the water. Do you think **the straw is empty** or do you think **the straw has something in it**?

   _____

4. Lower the straw into the water. Cover the top of the straw with your fingertip.

5. Lift the straw out of the water.

6. Keep the end of the straw covered and turn it upside down.

7. Turn the straw right side up again. Uncover the top of the straw.

8. Color the pictures to show what happened.

9. Why did it happen? Circle the true sentence.

   Air cannot be seen but it pushes and presses down on things.

   Air can be seen and it cannot push and press down on things.

Teacher: Tell the children air is present in a straw that appears empty. The water stays in its place as the covered straw is lifted from the cup and turned upside down. Tell the students that air is an invisible gas that is all around us. The weight of air pushing on things and pressing down is called **air pressure**. Air pressure holds the water in place and it also causes the water to drop from the straw.

Reproducible   © Fearon Teacher Aids FE11005

Record Sheet for _____ Date _____

Air Slows Things Down

Materials:

rock   8½" x 11" sheet of paper
coin   8½" x 11" piece of plastic
marble   8½" x 11" piece of cloth

Directions:

1. Write on the chart how you think each object will fall to the ground. Will it **fall straight down**? Will it **float sideways**?
2. Stand and drop each object. Watch each object fall.
3. Drop each object again. Watch to see if the objects fall the same way.
4. Write on the chart how each object fell to the ground.
5. Circle the true sentence.

   Small objects fall straight to the ground and big flat objects float as they fall.

   Small objects float as they fall and big flat objects fall straight to the ground.

Object	How will it fall?	How did it fall?
rock		
coin		
marble		
paper		
cloth		
plastic		

Teacher: Tell the children that air slows objects moving through it. Objects that are falling push against the air. Big things push against more air than little things do. As they fall to the ground, objects with larger surfaces have to push against more air so they float sideways before falling to the ground. Objects that are more compact have to push against less air so they fall straight to the ground.

© Fearon Teacher Aids FE11005   Reproducible

Record Sheet for _____ Date _____

Touch Bottom

Materials:

paper insect
toothpick
large bowl of water
short glass
crayons
piece of tape

Directions:

1. Color your insect. Tape it to a toothpick.

2. Place the insect on top of the water. Watch.

3. Does the insect **float** or **sink**? _____

4. Turn the glass upside down. Place it over the insect. When you place the glass on top of the water, you trap air inside of the glass.

5. Push the glass straight down to the bottom of the bowl. What happens? Draw a picture to show.

6. What could be pushing on the insect to keep it at the bottom of the bowl?

   _____

7. How long do you think a real insect could live like this?

   _____

8. Tilt the cup. What happens?

   _____

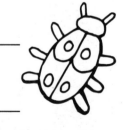

Teacher: To prepare for this experiment, reproduce Water Insects page 37 so each child has one insect to color. Tell the children that air is trapped inside the glass and that the trapped air pushes the water out of the way causing the insect to drop. Even though we cannot see air, it is there. (If air wasn't in the glass, the insect would not have been pushed to the bottom.) When the cup is tilted in the water, the water rushed in and the air escaped. A part of nature is to fill all spaces. Air takes up space and pushes on things.

Reproducible © Fearon Teacher Aids FE11005

Name _____ Date _____

Water Insects

Experimenting with air pressure

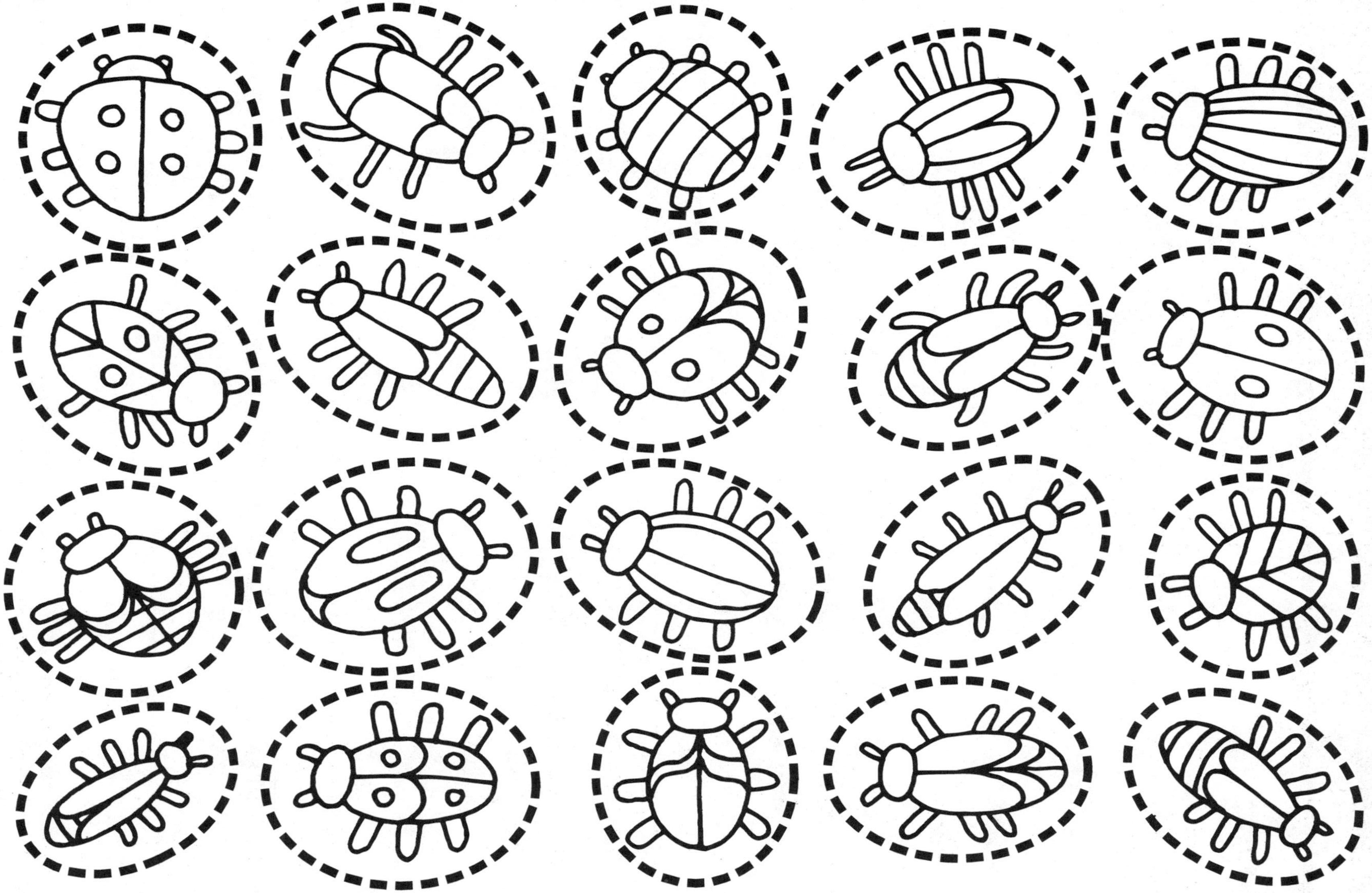

Teacher: Use this page with the experiment Touch Bottom on page 36. Reproduce this page so each child has at least one insect to color. Cut apart the insects and let each child choose an insect for the experiment. Have the students color their insects before doing the experiment.

© Fearon Teacher Aids FE11005

37

Reproducible

Record Sheet for _____ Date _____

Round and Round

Materials:

paper spinning wheel
pencil
glass of water
small pitcher

Directions:

1. Poke a pencil through the center dot of your spinning wheel.
2. Slide the wheel to the middle of the pencil.
3. Turn your wheel around and around so it moves easily on the pencil.
4. Hold the wheel. Does it move by itself? _____
5. Softly blow air on the wheel. What happens now?
   _____
6. Blow harder on the wheel. What happens this time?
   _____
7. Place the pencil on top of the glass. Make sure the wheel is over the water and is touching the water.
8. Does the wheel move by itself? _____
9. Blow air on the wheel. What happens now?
   _____
10. Pour the water into a small pitcher. Place the wheel on the empty cup. Slowly pour the water on one side of the wheel. What happens?
    _____

Teacher: Reproduce Spinning Wheels on page 39 on tagboard, one wheel for each student. Tell the children that when water or air is not moving, it has no **force**. Moving water and moving air have force and can do work. Machines can use water and air pressure to do work. The windmill, which is moved by air, can pump water out of the ground. A dam built in the path of moving water can do work. The moving water makes the turbines of generators inside the dam make electricity.

Name _____ Date _____

Spinning Wheels

Experimenting moving water and air

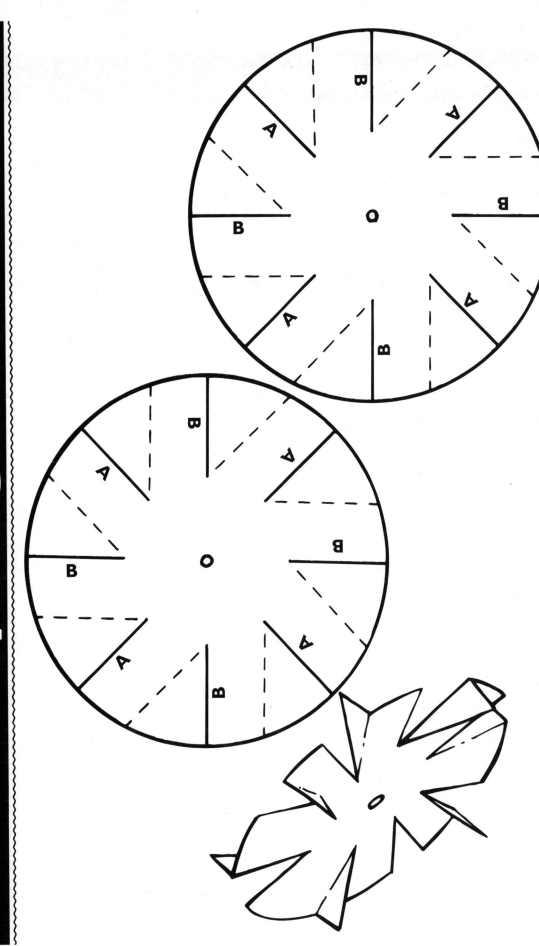

Teacher: Use this page with the experiment Round and Round on page 38. Reproduce this page on tagboard so each child has at least one spinning wheel. There are two patterns provided in case a child makes a mistake in cutting or folding the wheel. Have each student follow these directions: (1) Cut out the circle. (2) Cut along each solid line toward the center of the circle. (3) Fold on the dotted lines. Fold **A** lines **up**. Fold **B** lines **down**.

Record Sheet for _____ Date _____

Making a Siphon

Materials:

two clear plastic cups of water
24-inch length of plastic tubing
red and blue food coloring
pan or bucket with water

Directions:

1. Put two drops of red food coloring in one cup.

2. Put two drops of blue food coloring in the other cup.

3. Put the tube in the pan. Let the tube fill with water.

4. Put your finger over one end of the tube. Put the other end of the tube in the red cup of water. Keep your finger in place.

5. Without lifting your finger, put that end of the tube in the cup of blue water. Lift your finger. Does anything happen?

   _____

6. Lift the cup with the red water about five inches from the table. What happens? Color My Siphon Record Sheet to show what happens.

7. Now lift the cup with the blue water just a little above the table. What happens? Color My Siphon Record Sheet to show what happens.

Teacher: To prepare for this experiment, reproduce My Siphon Record Sheet on page 41. Make sure the plastic tube used is flexible. Have the children place the cups on a flat surface. Tell the children that by doing this experiment they made a **siphon**. A siphon transfers a liquid from one place to another. The two key parts of a siphon are (1) a tube with a bend and (2) two liquids at two different heights. Siphons are often used in irrigation to get water to the growing crops. This idea is even used to drain many water beds.

Reproducible   © Fearon Teacher Aids FE11005

Name _____ Date _____

My Siphon Record Sheet

Making a siphon. Recording observations

Color with a **red** crayon to show what happens to the red water.

Color with a **blue** crayon to show what happens to the blue water.

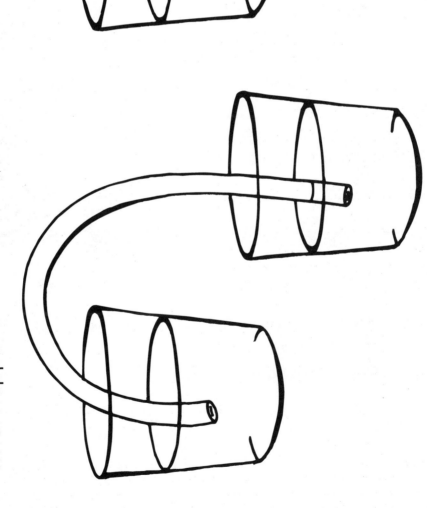

The water moves _____ .
fast   slowly

The water moves _____ .
fast   slowly

Teacher: Use this page with the experiment Making a Siphon on page 40. Have each student record what he or she observes by coloring in the diagrams on this sheet. Use this sheet also to help the students set up their siphons.

Record Sheet for _____   Date _____

Scrub-a-Dub Dub

Materials:

clear plastic cup half full of white vinegar
clear plastic cup with a spoonful of salt
old, tarnished penny
tablespoon

Directions:

1. Look at your penny. (Circle) the words that tell how it looks.

   shiny   dull   new   old   dirty   clean

2. Drop the penny into the salt cup. Pick it up. Brush off any salt on the penny.

   Does the penny look different? _____

3. Drop the penny in the vinegar cup. Get it out with a spoon.

   Does the penny look different? _____

4. Pour the salt into the vinegar cup. Mix it. Write what you think will happen to a penny if it is dropped in this mixture.

   _____
   _____
   _____

5. Put the penny in the salt and vinegar mixture. Use a spoon to take it out. Write how the penny changed.

   _____
   _____

Teacher: Tell the children that when a penny is dropped into just salt, there are no changes. When the penny is dropped into just the vinegar, there are no changes. But together salt and vinegar combine to form a substance that removes dirt and tarnish from pennies. You might let the students experiment with the salt and vinegar mixture to see if it removes dirt from other objects. Talk with the students about how they might use this mixture to clean other objects.

Record Sheet for _____ Date _____

Ice Cold

Materials:

three ice cubes
pie pan with water
string
salt
sand
paper towels

Directions:

1. Put the ice cubes in the water. On each cube lay one end of each string.
2. Cover one of the cubes with sand so the end of the string is covered too.
3. Cover one of the cubes with salt.
4. Count to 60.
5. Lift each string one at a time by the end not on the ice cube.
6. Write what happened when you lifted each string.

Ice Cube	What Happened?
sandy ice cube	
salty ice cube	
plain ice cube	

Teacher: To prepare for this experiment, have on hand ice cubes in a cooler to keep from melting. Cut three 8-inch lengths of string and fill a pie pan with water. Tell the children that salt is used on icy highways to help melt the ice quicker so vehicles can drive on them. Sand is also used on icy roads. The sand provides traction for car tires on the ice. Often salt and sand are mixed together and put on icy roads. The small amount of salt put on the ice cube and string melted the ice a little and the string was frozen in "new" ice that formed when the water refroze from the coldness. The salt helps the ice melt quicker. The coldness freezes the water. The string gets caught in the frozen water.

© Fearon Teacher Aids FE11005   Reproducible

Record Sheet for _____ Date _____

A Snappy Sound

Materials:

two thick rubber bands
two thin rubber bands
two small plastic bowls
two tin cans

Directions:

1. Stretch the thick rubber band over a bowl. Make it cross over the top of the bowl. Pluck the rubber band. What can you hear?

   _____

2. Pluck the rubber band again. What can you see it do?

   _____

3. Pluck the rubber band again. Quickly touch it with your finger. What happens?

   _____

4. Stretch the thin rubber band over the other bowl. Make it cross over the top of the bowl. Pluck the rubber band. What can you hear?

   _____

5. Is the sound **higher** or **lower** than the sound of the thick rubber band?

   _____

6. Stretch a thick rubber band over a bowl. Stretch a thin rubber band over the other bowl. Pluck each. Which rubber band makes a higher sound?

   _____

Teacher: Tell the children that a rubber band shakes (**vibrates**) when it is plucked. The pitch of the rubber band is determined by its thickness, its length, the distance its stretched, and the number of times it vibrates. Musical instruments such as guitars, pianos, and banjos have strings or wires of varying thicknesses to produce high and low sounds. A guitar player changes the pitch by changing the length of the strings by holding down the strings on different frets along the neck of the instrument while playing. The piano is also made with strings of varying lengths. Challenge the children to decide which rubber bands make the highest pitch when plucked—the one over the can or the one over the bowl. The sounds of the rubber bands are influenced by what objects they are stretched over.

Record Sheet for _____ Date _____

Sound Travels

Materials:

two paper cups
two paper clips
length of string
pencil

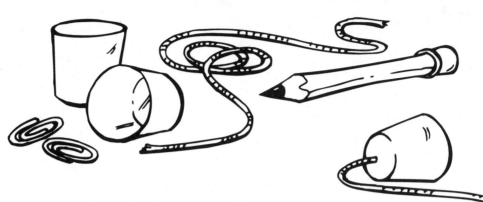

Directions:

1. Use a pencil to poke a hole in the bottom of each cup.

2. Thread the ends of the string through the holes from the outside to the inside.

3. Tie each end of the string to a paper clip to keep the string from slipping back through the hole.

4. Work with a friend. Hold one cup. Have your friend hold the other cup. Stand apart from each other so the string is pulled tight. Hold the cup to your ear. Have your friend speak into the other cup. Switch roles. Write what happens.

   _____
   _____

5. Stand closer to your friend so the string hangs loose. Take turns talking into the cups. Write what happens.

   _____
   _____

6. Do you think your "simple telephone" would work without the string? _____

Teacher: To prepare for this experiment, cut a 20-foot length of thin string. Tell the children that sound is made when an object **vibrates** (moves quickly back and forth) and causes the surrounding air to vibrate. Sound travels through air, water, and solid objects such as wood, wire, and string. Sound spreads out in all directions. When the **vibrations** reach our ears, we hear sound. The farther sound waves travel and the more they spread, the more difficult they are for us to hear. So the nearer a sound is to us the louder it sounds to us. You might have the students gather other materials (plastic cups, yarn, etc.) and try to make "simple telephones."

Record Sheet for _____ Date _____

Sound Waves

Materials:

megaphone
watch
glass of water

Directions:

1. Lay the watch at one end of a table. Put your ear at the other end of the table. Does the ticking sound **loud** or **soft**?

   _____

2. Move the watch to the middle of the table. Does the ticking sound the **same**, **louder**, or **softer**?

   _____

3. Hold the megaphone to your ear. Does the ticking sound the **same**, **louder**, or **softer**?

   _____

4. Place the watch next to one side of the glass of water. Hold it against the glass. Put your ear against the other side of the glass. Listen. Do you hear a ticking sound?

   _____

5. Lay the watch on the table. Put your ear on top of the table. Plug your other ear with your finger. Listen. Do you hear a ticking sound?

   _____

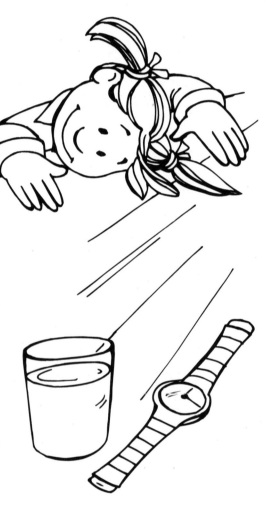

Teacher: To prepare for this experiment, roll a sheet of posterboard into a cone and secure with brass fasteners or tape to make a **megaphone**. The children will also need a loud-ticking wrist watch or clock. Tell the children that sound spreads out in waves in all directions. The farther **sound waves** travel and the more they spread, the more difficult it is to hear the sound. The megaphone directs the sound waves into a more direct path to our ear. This helps us hear the sound better. Our outer ear collects the sound waves and directs the sound to our ear drum to help us hear. Sound travels through air, water, wood, and along wires and string.

Reproducible   © Fearon Teacher Aids FE11005

Record Sheet for _____ Date _____

The Blob

Materials:

ball of "blob"
plastic cup
large spoon
sheet of wax paper

Directions:

1. Put the blob in the cup. Stir it with your finger. Poke it. Smell it.

2. Write what it feels and smells like.

   It feels _____.

   It smells _____.

3. Try to pour the blob onto the wax paper. Does it pour like a liquid or keep its shape like a solid?
   _____
   _____

4. Make a ball out of the blob. Try these things.

   Will it roll? _____

   Will it bounce? _____

   Will it flatten like a pancake? _____

5. If you were to give the blob a name, what would you call it? Why?

   I would name it _____ because
   _____
   _____.

Teacher: To prepare for this experiment, mix cornstarch, water, and food coloring into the consistency of toothpaste to make the "blob." Each child will experiment with a small ball of the substance (about 3 to 5 tablespoons). Have the children wear old clothes or a smock when doing this experiment. Tell the children that this strange substance acts like both a liquid and a solid. When it is rolled into a ball, it acts like a solid and keeps its shape. But when it is in the cup it acts like a liquid because it takes the shape of the container instead of keeping its own shape. Other mixtures such as peanut butter and milk shakes can also behave both like a solid and a liquid.

© Fearon Teacher Aids FE11005   Reproducible

Record Sheet for _____ Date _____

Colorful Clay

Materials:

three balls of clay (red, yellow, blue)
crayons

Directions:

1. Make three tiny balls out of each of the large balls of clay.

2. Take a tiny yellow ball and a tiny blue ball. If you mix them together, would you get **orange**, **green**, or **purple**?
   _____

3. Mix them together into one ball. What color did they make?
   _____

4. Take a tiny yellow ball and a tiny red ball. If you mix them together, would you get **orange**, **green**, or **purple**? _____

5. Mix them together into one ball. What color did they make?
   _____

6. Take a tiny red ball and a tiny blue ball. If you mix them together, would you get **orange**, **green**, or **purple**? _____

7. Mix them together into one ball. What color did they make?
   _____

8. Use crayons to color My Color Wheel.

9. Roll each ball of clay into a snake shape. Pinch off pieces and make a rainbow snake in this order—red, orange, yellow, green, blue, purple. Name your snake!

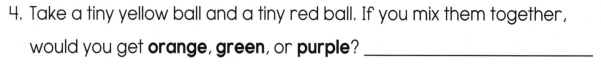

Teacher: To prepare for this experiment, make three small balls of clay—one red, one blue, and one yellow—for each child. Reproduce My Color Wheel record sheet on page 49 for each child. Tell the children that red, yellow, and blue are called **primary colors** because they can be mixed to create almost every other color or shade of color. By mixing primary colors together we can create orange, green, and purple. Orange, green, and purple are called **secondary colors** because they are created by two steps—creating primary colors and then mixing two primary colors.

Name _____ Date _____

My Color Wheel

Color wheel, primary and secondary colors

Color the **red**, **yellow**, and **blue** circles. These are **primary colors**. What two colors make **orange**? What two colors make **green**? What two colors make **purple**? These are **secondary colors**. Color these circles. Label each circle.

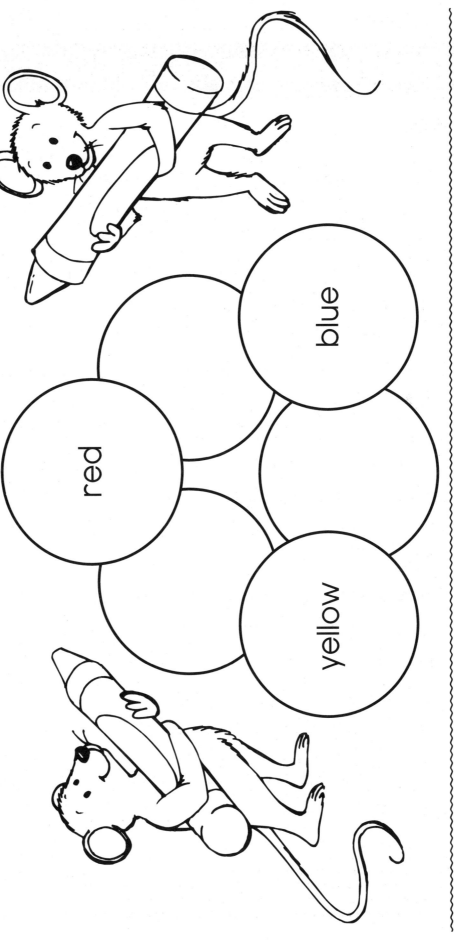

Teacher: Use this page with the experiment Colorful Clay on page 48. Have each student color the red, yellow, and blue primary color circles first. Then review with the students what two colors make orange (red and yellow), what two colors make green (yellow and blue), and what two colors make purple (red and blue). Have the students write these secondary color names inside the matching circles.

© Fearon Teacher Aids FE11005

49

Reproducible

Record Sheet for _____ Date _____

A Good Chance

Materials:

red marble
blue marble
paper lunch bag

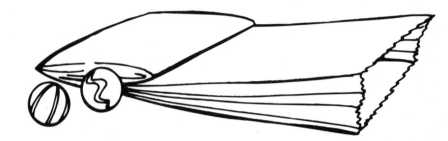

Directions:

1. Put the marbles inside the bag.

2. Put your hand in the bag.

3. Without looking, pull out a marble.

4. What color is it? Mark your answer by making an **X** in the correct column after Try #1 on My Chance Record sheet.

5. Put the marble back in the bag.

6. Without looking pull out a marble again. What color is it? Mark your answer by making an **X** in the correct column after Try #2 on My Chance Record sheet.

7. Repeat this activity 18 more times to complete the record sheet.

8. When you are done, answer these questions:

   How many times did you pull out a blue marble? _____

   How many times did you pull out a red marble? _____

Teacher: To prepare for this experiment, reproduce My Chance Record sheet on page 51 for each child. Tell the children that **probability** means the chance or possibility of things happening. Two things can happen in this experiment—a red marble can be pulled out or a blue marble can be pulled out of the bag. Since there is only one red marble out of a possible two marbles, we have one chance in two to get a red marble. The probability of getting a red marble is "1 in 2." This is sometimes written "1:2" or "1/2." Each of these ways of writing a probability is called a **ratio**. If we do this experiment 20 times, the probability is we would pull out the red marble 10 times. This doesn't mean that is what has to happen. It means there's a good chance it will happen. Probability helps us in life by telling us the chance of something happening so we can make wise choices. For example, the chance of getting hurt in an automobile accident without wearing your seat belt is larger than your chance of getting hurt badly wearing your seat belt. By knowing these chances, we can wisely choose to wear our seat belts.

Reproducible © Fearon Teacher Aids FE11005

Name _____ Date _____

My Chance Record

Probability

# Try	Blue Marble	Red Marble
#1		
#2		
#3		
#4		
#5		
#6		
#7		
#8		
#9		
#10		

# Try	Blue Marble	Red Marble
#11		
#12		
#13		
#14		
#15		
#16		
#17		
#18		
#19		
#20		

Teacher: Use this page with the experiment A Good Chance on page 50. Have each child mark an **X** under the correct column to show whether a blue marble or a red marble was pulled from the bag. Next to Try #1 have each child reach into his or her bag and without looking pull out a marble. Next to Try #1 have each child mark an **X** under the correct column to show whether a blue marble or a red marble was pulled from the bag. Have the students repeat this 20 times all together. Remind the students to put the pulled-out marble back into the bag before each try.

© Fearon Teacher Aids FE11005

Reproducible

Record Sheet for _____ Date _____

Weighing In

Materials:

scale
box of paper clips
50 pennies
objects for weighing (pencil, eraser, rock, ping pong ball)

Directions:

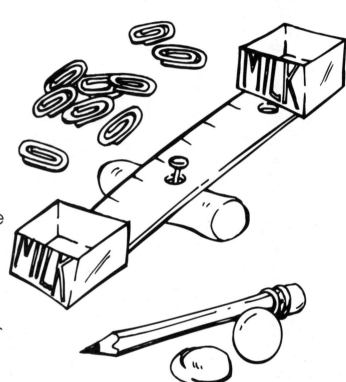

1. Look at My Weight Chart. Read the list of objects to be weighed.

2. How many paper clips do you think would equal the weight of each object? Write each guess on My Weight Chart.

3. Take the first object listed and place it on one end of the scale. Add paper clips to the other end of the scale until the two ends are level or balanced. Write how many paper clips the object "weighs." Write your answer on My Weight Chart. Do this for each object.

4. How many pennies do you think would equal the weight of each object? Write each guess on My Weight Chart.

5. Repeat step 3 with each object. Use pennies to "weigh" each object. Remember to write your answers on My Weight Chart.

Teacher: To prepare for this experiment, reproduce My Weight Chart on page 53 for each child. Gather simple items for the students to weigh—short pencil, long pencil, pencil eraser, chalkboard eraser, piece of chalk, scissors, rock, small rubber ball, ping pong ball. If you don't have a simple scale to weigh objects you can make one by following these directions: (1) Cut two half-pint milk cartons in half. (2) Tape one cut milk carton on each end of a ruler that has a center hole. (3) Roll a ball of clay into a thick column. (4) Lay the center of the ruler on the column of clay and push a nail through the hole into the clay. This should secure the ruler in the clay. Tell the children weighing is one way we can learn about something or compare two different things. To compare weights, we need to compare everything we want to weigh to a **standard unit**. In this experiment, the first "standard unit" of weight is paper clips and the second "standard unit" of weight is pennies. The most common standard units of weight are **pounds** and **grams**.

Reproducible

Name _____ Date _____

My Weight Chart

Comparing weights of objects, estimating

Objects	Paper Clips		Objects	Pennies	
	Guess	Actual		Guess	Actual

Teacher: Use this page with the experiment Weighing In on page 52. Gather simple items for the students to weigh—short pencil, long pencil, pencil eraser, chalkboard eraser, piece of chalk, scissors, rock, small rubber ball, ping pong ball. Write the name of each object you want the students to weigh on the chart. Then reproduce the chart for each child. Let the children use a simple scale for weighing or see the directions at the bottom of page 52 for making a simple scale that the children can use.

© Fearon Teacher Aids FE11005   Reproducible

Record Sheet for _____ Date _____

Coasting Downhill

Materials:

three books
two small toy cars (one bigger than the other one)
cardboard strip
carpet strip
wooden block
sheet of sandpaper

Directions:

1. Pile the books together on a table. Place one end of the cardboard strip on top of the pile to make a ramp.

2. Put both cars side by side at the top of the cardboard ramp. Let them roll. Circle the speed of each car.

   Smaller Car   fast   medium   slow
   Bigger Car   fast   medium   slow

3. Lay the carpet strip on top of the cardboard.

4. Put both cars side by side at the top of the carpet ramp. Let them roll. Circle the speed of each car.

   Smaller Car   fast   medium   slow
   Bigger Car   fast   medium   slow

5. Feel the wood block. Rub the sandpaper over the block while counting to 30.

6. Does the block feel **warmer** or **cooler**? _____

Teacher: To prepare for this experiment, collect small toy cars of different sizes. Ask a local carpet dealer for some carpet scraps or samples. Cut a wide strip of corrugated cardboard that will support the weight of two cars and that is wide enough to allow both of the cars side by side to roll down it. Cut the carpet sample so it is the same size as the cardboard strip. Ask a local lumber dealer to cut you a block of wood from a scrap of lumber. Tell the students that everything is made up of **molecules**. When the molecules of two objects meet, **friction** occurs. The amount of friction depends on the texture of the two objects. The smooth tires on the toy cars rolling on the smooth cardboard does not cause very much friction. The carpeted ramp causes more friction to occur so the toy cars roll slower. The same thing happens with the sandpaper. When the two surfaces of the wood and sandpaper meet, friction occurs and produces heat.

Record Sheet for _____ Date _____

Rolling Down a Ramp

Materials:

ping pong ball
tiny rubber ball
ruler
masking tape
scissors
three books

Directions:

1. Place a book on a table. Place one end of the ruler on top of the book and the other end next to the edge of table. This makes a ramp.

2. Put the ping pong ball at the top of the ramp. Let it go. Watch where it lands! Mark the spot with a piece of tape. Write **P1** on the tape.

3. Now put the rubber ball at the top of the ramp. Let it go. Watch where it lands! Mark the spot with a piece of tape. Write **J1** on the tape.

4. Put another book on top of the first book to make the ramp higher.

5. Do step 2. Write **P2** on the tape.

6. Do step 3. Write **J2** on the tape.

7. Put the third book on top of the other books to make the ramp even higher.

8. Do step 2. Write **P3** on the tape.

9. Do step 3. Write **J3** on the tape.

10. Which ball traveled the farthest from the table—**P1, P2, P3, J1, J2, J3**? _____

11. Which ball traveled the shortest distance—**P1, P2, P3, J1, J2, J3**? _____

Teacher: To prepare for this experiment, collect a ping pong ball, a jacks' rubber ball, a ruler with a groove down the center, and three books about the same thickness. Tell the students that the higher a ramp is, the more speed a ball gains as it rolls down the ramp. The high speed allows the ball to travel farther away from the table. But if the ramp is straight up and down, the rolling ball will go fast but will fall straight down instead of traveling far from the table. Since a small rubber ball weighs more than a ping pong ball, it takes longer to build up speed. The ping pong ball will travel faster quicker. It also takes heavier objects longer to stop than lighter weight objects going the same speed. Because of this, a train traveling 15 miles per hour usually cannot stop for something in its way, whereas a car going the same speed (the car being lighter weight than the train) has a better chance of stopping before hitting an obstacle.

© Fearon Teacher Aids FE11005 — Reproducible

Record Sheet for _____ Date _____

Levers

Materials:

ruler
ball of clay
rock
sheet of wax paper

Directions:

1. Roll the clay into a thick snake on the wax paper.
2. Put the clay under the center of the ruler.
3. Lay the rock on one end of the ruler. Gently push down the other end of the ruler. What happens?

   _____

4. Roll the clay closer to one end of the ruler. Lay the rock on the opposite end of the ruler. Gently push down the other end of the ruler. Is it **easier** or **harder** to lift the rock?

   _____

5. Roll the clay even closer to one end of the ruler. Lay the rock on the opposite end. Gently push down the other end of the ruler. Is it **easier** or **harder** to lift the rock?

   _____

6. Look at the pictures on My Lever Chart. Which picture shows an **easy** way to lift the rock? Which picture shows a **harder** way? Which shows the **hardest** way? Record your answers on My Lever Chart.

Teacher: To prepare for this experiment, show the children how to roll a ball of clay into a 1-inch thick column or "snake." Demonstrate how to find the center of a ruler (the 6-inch mark). Reproduce My Lever Chart on page 57 for each student. Tell the children that a **lever** is a simple machine that is used in many ways to make work easier. In this experiment, the ball of clay is the **fulcrum**. A fulcrum is the support and the point from which everything else moves. The fulcrum does not move. Pushing on one end of the lever is called the **force**. The rock on the other end of the lever is called the **load**. This type of lever is a **first class lever**. First class levers are things like teeter-totters and crowbars.

Reproducible 56 © Fearon Teacher Aids FE11005

Name _____ Date _____

Working with levers

My Lever Chart

Which picture shows an **easy** way to lift a rock. Which picture shows a **harder** way? Which picture shows the **hardest** way? Label each picture.

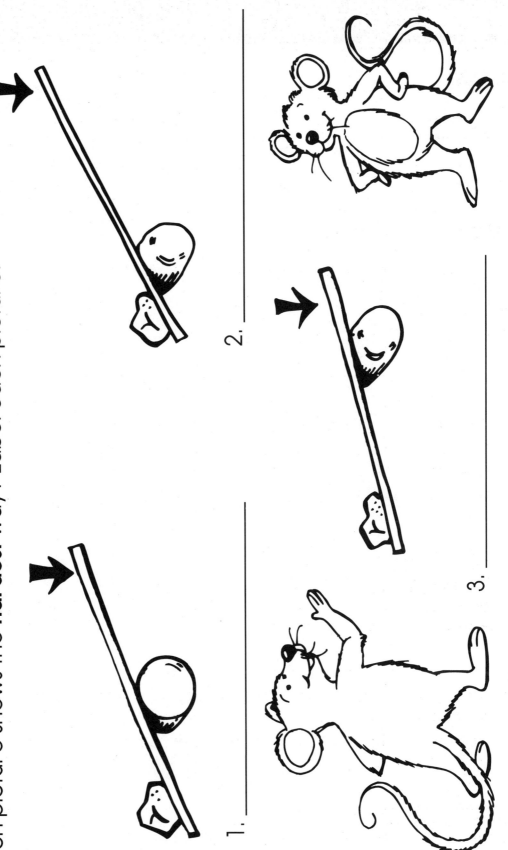

Teacher: Use this page with the experiment Levers on page 56. Reproduce this chart for each student. Have each student label the pictures using the words **easy, harder, hardest.**

© Fearon Teacher Aids FE11005

57

Reproducible

Record Sheet for _____ Date _____

Let There Be Light

Materials:

D battery
small flashlight bulb
insulated copper wire
masking tape
aluminum foil
paper clips

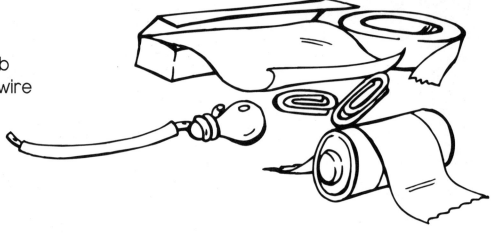

Directions:

1. Tape the battery to a table. Twist one end of the wire around the metal bottom of the bulb.

2. Connect the items as shown in each picture. Answer each question.

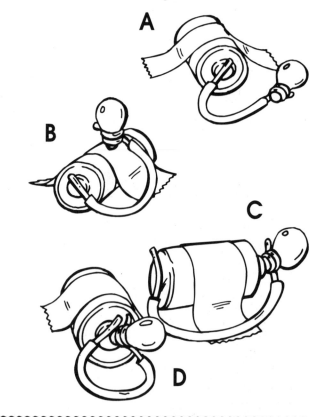

Picture A: Does the bulb light up? _____

Picture B: Does the bulb light up? _____

Picture C: Does the bulb light up? _____

Picture D: Does the bulb light up? _____

Teacher: To prepare for this experiment, collect a D-size battery (1.5 volts), 12 inches of insulated copper wire (scrape each of the coated ends with scissors to expose some of the bare wire), and a small flashlight bulb (2.5 volts). Tell the students that **current electricity** needs a complete loop or circle-like path to flow into things and make them work. The circular path that electricity flows along is called an **electric circuit**. An electric circuit has three parts—a source of electricity, a device that uses the electricity, and a conductor between the two. In order for a flashlight bulb to light we need to have a complete circuit.

Record Sheet for _____ Date _____

Stuck on You

Materials:

6-volt dry cell battery
iron nail
insulated copper wire
small metal paper clips

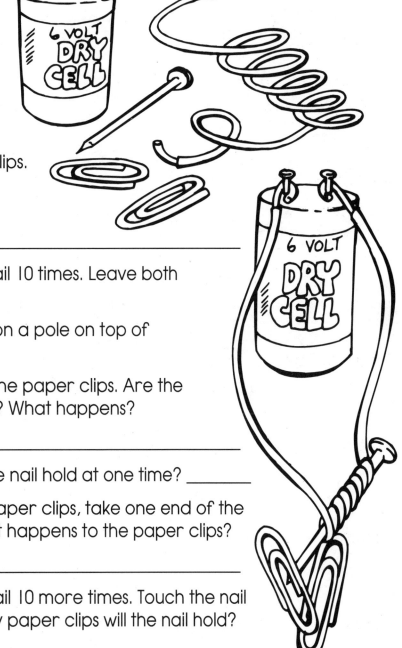

Directions:

1. Touch the nail to the paper clips. Does the nail hold them? What happens?

   _____

2. Wrap the wire around the nail 10 times. Leave both ends of the wire loose.

3. Wrap each end of the wire on a pole on top of the battery.

4. Touch the end of the nail to the paper clips. Are the paper clips pulled to the nail? What happens?

   _____

5. How many paper clips will the nail hold at one time? _____

6. While the nail is holding the paper clips, take one end of the wire off of the battery. What happens to the paper clips?

   _____

7. Wrap the wire around the nail 10 more times. Touch the nail to the paper clips. How many paper clips will the nail hold?

   _____

Teacher: To prepare for this experiment, collect a 6-volt dry cell battery, one yard of insulated copper wire (scrape each of the coated ends with scissors to expose some of the bare wire), small metal paper clips, and a large iron nail (e.g. 20 common). Tell the students when wire is connected to both terminals of a battery, a complete circuit is created. The electrical energy that flows through the wire turns the wire and nail into an **electromagnet**. The amount of **magnetism** increases by adding more turns of the wire around the nail and by the amount of electrical energy used (the size and number of batteries). Occasionally even after the wire has been disconnected, the nail may retain a small amount of magnetism for a short period of time.

© Fearon Teacher Aids FE11005   Reproducible

Super Scientist

AWARD presented to

by _____ Date _____

Science Wizard

AWARD presented to

by _____ Date _____

Teacher: Reproduce class sets of these awards and use them to honor each of your young scientists after completing one or more of the experiments in this book. Let the children color their awards and take them home to share with their families.

Reproducible   © Fearon Teacher Aids FE11005